AF228917

US ARMED FORCES

NAVY SEALS

KENNY ABDO

Fly!
An Imprint of Abdo Zoom
abdobooks.com

abdobooks.com

Published by Abdo Zoom, a division of ABDO, P.O. Box 398166, Minneapolis, Minnesota 55439. Copyright © 2019 by Abdo Consulting Group, Inc. International copyrights reserved in all countries. No part of this book may be reproduced in any form without written permission from the publisher. Fly!™ is a trademark and logo of Abdo Zoom.

Printed in China.
092018
012019

Photo Credits: Alamy, Everett Collection, iStock, Shutterstock, ©US Navy
Production Contributors: Kenny Abdo, Jennie Forsberg, Grace Hansen
Design Contributors: Dorothy Toth, Neil Klinepier

Library of Congress Control Number: 2018946327

Publisher's Cataloging-in-Publication Data

Names: Abdo, Kenny, author.
Title: Navy SEALs / by Kenny Abdo.
Description: Minneapolis, Minnesota : Abdo Zoom, 2019 | Series: US Armed
    Forces | Includes online resources and index.
Identifiers: ISBN 9781532125492 (lib. bdg.) | ISBN 9781641856942 (pbk) |
    ISBN 9781532126512 (ebook) | ISBN 9781532127021 (Read-to-me ebook)
Subjects: LCSH: SEALs (Military unit)--Juvenile literature. | United States. Navy--
    Operations specialists--Juvenile literature. | Special force troops--Juvenile
    literature. | Military departments and divisions--United States--Juvenile
    literature.
Classification: DDC 359.9--dc23

TABLE OF CONTENTS

NAVY SEALS

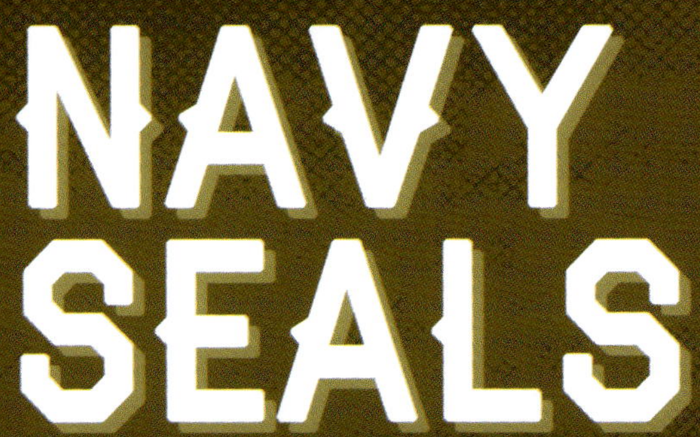

Whether it's rising from the ocean, jumping out of an airplane, or kicking in doors—the United States Navy SEALs are ready for it all.

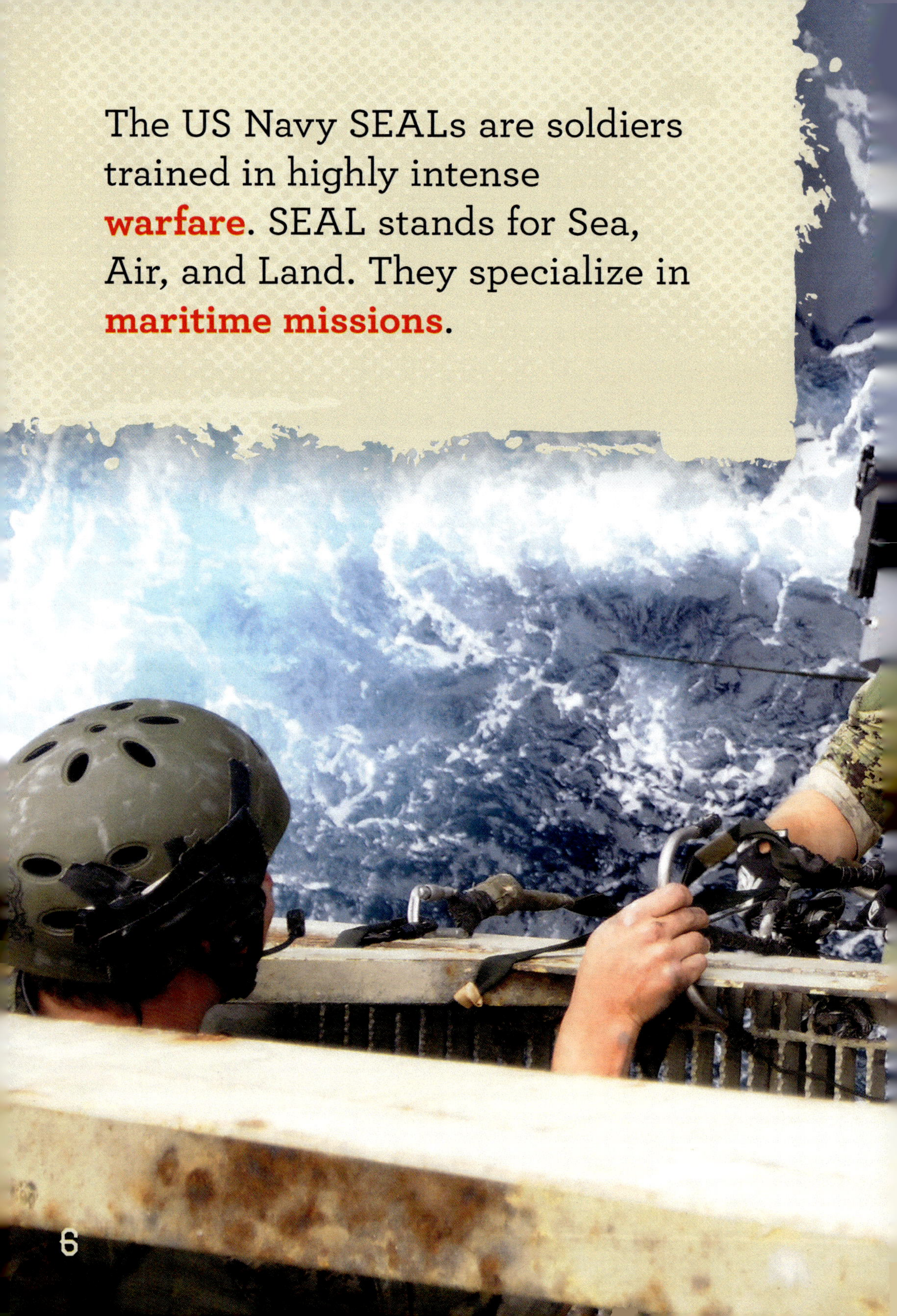

The US Navy SEALs are soldiers trained in highly intense **warfare**. SEAL stands for Sea, Air, and Land. They specialize in **maritime missions**.

INTEL

The first US Navy SEAL team came together in **World War II**. They were called the Scouts and Raiders. They were formed nine months after the attack on **Pearl Harbor**.

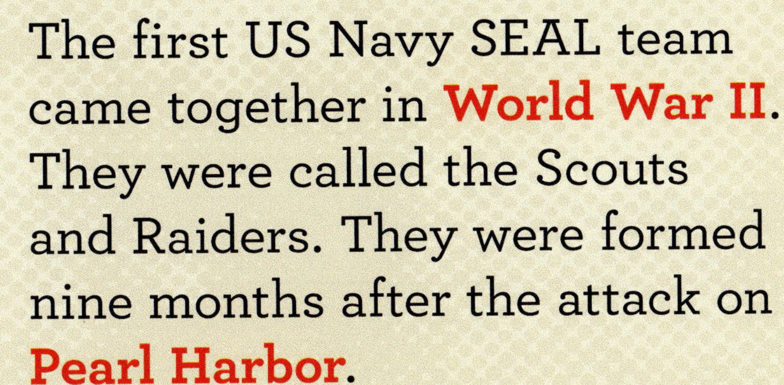

President John F. Kennedy officially revealed the Navy SEAL force in 1962. He thought they would be useful during the **Cold War**.

11

Training to become a SEAL is so intense, more than 80% of recruits quit before it is over.

Navy SEALs make up less than 1% of the US Navy. The small number of specially trained SEALs are able to complete certain **missions** that larger forces cannot.

IN ACTION

SEALs are trained to work in desert, jungle, and urban settings. They can parachute into action, use almost any weapon, and are taught to survive intense torture.

Monday
StarTribune
RTRIBUNE.COM: YOUR BREAKING NEWS SOURCE • MINNESOTA'S TOP NEWS CHOICE • MINNEAPOLIS, ST. PAUL • MAY 2, 20

"Justice has been done."

PRESIDENT OBAMA

BIN LADEN IS DEAD

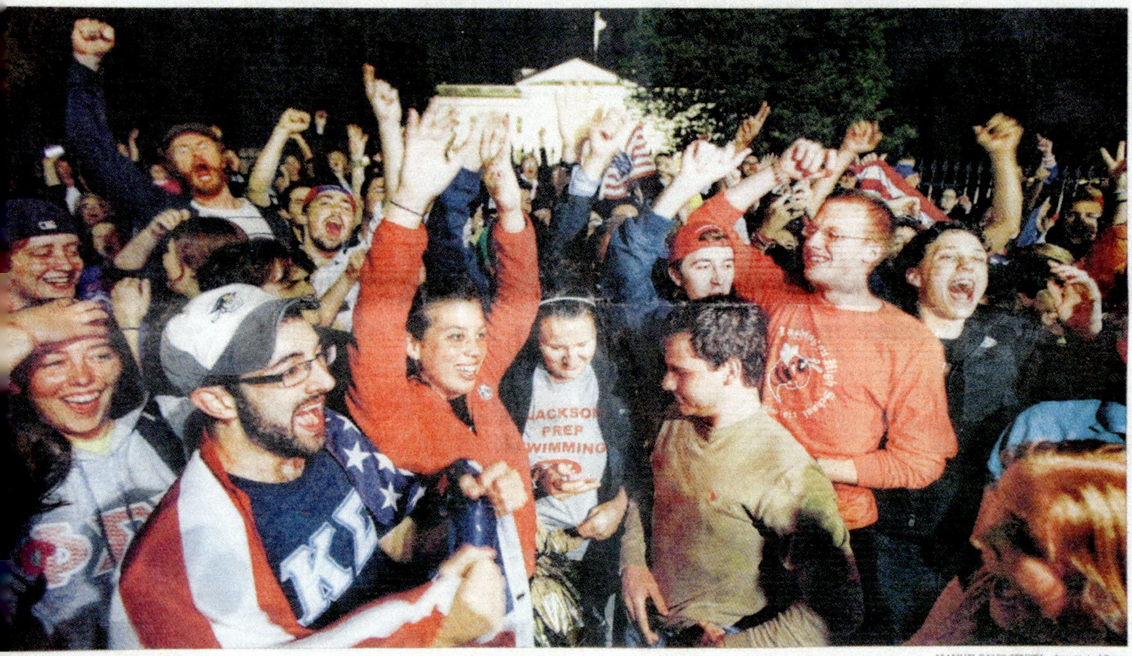

MANUEL BALSE CENETA • Associated Press

crowd cheered Sunday outside the White House upon hearing the news that Al-Qaida leader Osama bin Laden had been killed. President Obama said a U.S. team had "taken custody of his body."

American team kills terrorist in Pakistan

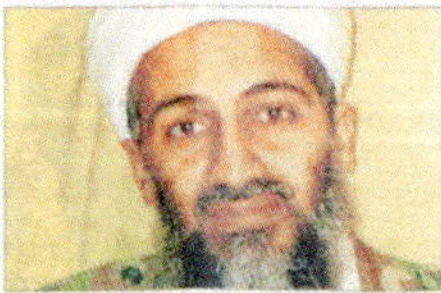

He was world's face of terror

- Bin Laden built a global terrorist network responsible for 9/11 and other attacks, but eluded capture for two decades.

There are 10 SEAL teams that are **deployed** worldwide. SEAL Team 6 is the most recognized for taking down Osama Bin Laden.

UNIT

The Belgian Malinois are the dogs of the Navy SEALs. They have a sense of smell over 40 times greater than humans, and are twice as fast. They also skydive into **missions** with SEAL teams.

GLOSSARY

Cold War – a time of political tension between the Eastern and Western countries of the world between 1947 and 1991.

deploy – the act of moving soldiers into a position of action.

maritime – military activity on the sea.

mission – an important job carried out by the armed forces.

Pearl Harbor – a military base in Hawaii that was attacked during World War II.

recruit – a person who joins the armed forces.

warfare – the actions involved in war.

World War II – a war fought in Europe, Asia, and Africa from 1939 to 1945.

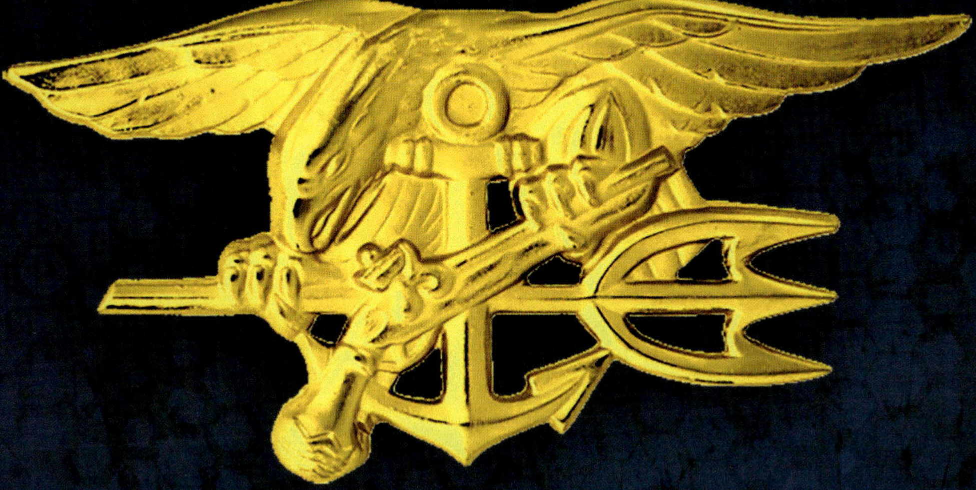

ONLINE RESOURCES

To learn more about the Navy SEALs, please visit **abdobooklinks.com**. These links are routinely monitored and updated to provide the most current information available.

INDEX